EUCHARIST AS WORD

Lectio Divina
and the Eucharist

MICHEL DE VERTEUIL CSSP

VERITAS

First published 2001 by
Veritas Publications
7/8 Lower Abbey Street
Dublin 1
Ireland

Email publications@veritas.ie
Website www.veritas.ie

ISBN 1 85390 519 4

A catalogue record for this book is available from the British
Library.

Cover design by Bill Bolger
Printed in the Republic of Ireland by Betaprint Ltd,
Dublin

Veritas books are printed on paper made from the wood pulp
of managed forests. For every tree felled, at least one tree is
planted, thereby renewing natural resources.

CONTENTS

INTRODUCTION

This book is divided into two sections, each of them a response to a local situation that I later discovered to be widespread.

The first comes from the nineties, when the Church in the Caribbean was preparing for a Eucharistic Congress in Trinidad. As always happens with these Congresses, the bishops of the region, the Antilles Episcopal Conference, turned it into an opportunity for catechesis on the Eucharist.

As the time for the Congress approached however, I was more and more struck by the fact that many Catholics – including some of the most fervent – were largely unaware of the rich insights on the Eucharist that had emerged at the Second Vatican Council. Their devotion to the Eucharist seemed to be what it was before that great event. I realised then that the teachings of the Council had not filtered down to the rank and file of the Church, or had remained so much on the surface that they were now largely forgotten.

This was particularly sad for me, as I had lived through the period of the Council as a young priest, and remembered well the liturgical renewal that preceded and followed it; it was a time of tremendous enthusiasm and hope; it marked us for ever.

The Conciliar Fathers had themselves seen the danger of the momentum being lost. The *Document on the Liturgy* includes this warning: 'There is no hope of achieving liturgical renewal unless pastors of souls, in the first place themselves, become fully imbued with the spirit and power of the liturgy and attain competence in it' (No. 14). The *Document* went on to challenge priests: 'With diligence and patience pastors of souls should see to the liturgical instruction of the faithful and their active participation, internal and external, in the liturgy' (No. 19).

I decided then to exercise my own 'diligence and patience' by writing a series of articles on the Eucharist for our archdiocesan weekly newspaper, the *Catholic News*, incorporating the insights of the Council and of the liturgical renewal. Many found the articles helpful, so I am pleased to offer them here to a wider audience.

Teaching the faith to others always leads to growth in one's own faith. In this case too, my insights became clearer over the several months during which the articles were written. I hope that readers will discern this growing clarity amid a certain amount of repetition.

The second part of the book arose from a pastoral problem with the Sunday Lectionary. One of the most important conciliar reforms was to restore the ancient practice of 'continuous reading' (*lectio continua*) of the gospel. This is now done during the Sundays of Ordinary Time when one of the Synoptic Gospels is read over a year in a three-year cycle.

A problem arose in year two, however, when the gospel is St Mark's. His being the shortest of the Synoptics, the framers of the lectionary found that there were not enough passages to fill the thirty-four Sundays of Ordinary Time. They decided then that in July-August the continuous reading would be interrupted and, for five consecutive Sundays, from the seventeenth to the twenty-first Sunday in Ordinary Time, the gospel texts would be a continuous reading of St John, chapter 6 – Jesus as the bread of life.

I have always thought that this pragmatic decision turned out to be a marvellous grace for the Church, an opportunity for local communities in every part of the world to make a prolonged meditation on the Eucharist, using Jesus' own teaching method. After a time, however, I realised that many homilists were not experiencing the texts in that positive way. They were finding these gospel readings repetitive and even boring – 'another teaching on the Eucharist!'

In order to help homilists profit from this time of grace, I decided to propose (again in the *Catholic News*) a series of meditations for each Sunday of that sequence.

Both these experiences brought home to me once more the teaching of the Council that the liturgy is the best setting for popular theological education, as it was in the first centuries of the Church's history. The liturgical setting has several effects:

- Theology is based on bible reading
- It is integrated into prayer, including contemplative prayer
- It is concerned with the real life situation of the local community
- It is done in communion with the worldwide Church community.

The liturgical setting explains why, in those first centuries, theologians were generally pastors, preachers and mystics. A return to this state of affairs is a valuable and challenging goal for theology today. My hope is that this book will, in some small way, facilitate the process.

I wish to express my sincere thanks to Fr Brendan Clifford OP, my long-standing friend and colleague in the biblical apostolate. That this little work was finally brought to completion is largely due to his encouragement – and unfailing patience.

PART I

1

TEACHING BY SIGNS

A Eucharistic Congress is a moment of grace for our Church. It gives us the opportunity, as a Church Community, to become more aware of the great treasure that we have in the Eucharist. There are many aspects that we can look at but one is basic – Jesus chose to make himself present to us 'under the species of bread and wine', as our traditional Catholic teaching puts it.

The Eucharist, like all the sacraments of the Church, is not merely a source of grace, it is also a pedagogy, a way of teaching. When we meet Jesus in a sacrament, we both meet him and at the same time learn something about him. That is the way sacraments work, they teach us even as we celebrate them.

Applying this principle to the Eucharist, the particular way in which Jesus invites us to meet him is in the species of bread and wine. Doing this must not be secondary, but central, to our meeting. If we by-pass the species and, as it were, go directly to him, we are not entering fully into the Eucharist and our meeting with him is not as enriching as it should be.

We must go further: in the Eucharist we meet Jesus, not primarily under the species of bread and wine in themselves, but as bread that we eat and a cup of wine from which we drink. Here is the primary wonder of the Eucharist, this way in which God-in-Jesus has made himself present to us. It reveals the nature of our God. He whom humanity in every culture has tended to locate somewhere up in the skies, or in an awe-inspiring temple, is present to us in this extraordinary humble way.

The Eucharist, understood in this way, is also an example to be imitated, 'I have given you an example so that you may copy what I have done to you' (John 13:15); 'This is my commandment, love one another as I have loved you' (John 15:2). The Eucharist teaches us something that spouses, parents and teachers know well from their own experience – that love does not consist primarily of giving things, but of giving ourselves to be consumed by others. The Eucharist invites us to recognise and celebrate that our flesh is real food and our blood real drink, and only if we let them eat our flesh and drink our blood will they live in us and we live in them (John 6:55-56).

There are other treasures to be discovered in the Eucharistic presence of Jesus. By the process that we call assimilation, when we eat food it becomes us. It is something of the same when we receive the Eucharist. If, after communion, we ask the question 'Where is Jesus?', the answer is that he is now present in the people. He has given up his own countenance and taken on their varied countenances. These countenances are deformed perhaps, or scarred by poverty or domestic violence, or simply by heartbreak, but they are now the only countenance of Christ and when we welcome them – or the truth of ourselves – we welcome him.

Once again the Eucharist is teaching us something very important about Jesus; he gives himself to us in this way. A popular hymn has him saying, 'lose yourself in me and you find yourself'. This isn't mere theory, Jesus does it himself in the Eucharist, losing himself and finding himself in us. In the Eucharist, he also puts into practice his other teaching, 'Unless a wheat grain falls into the earth and dies, it remains only a single grain, but if it dies it yields a rich harvest' (John 12:24).

In this way, too, the Eucharist teaches us how to love, 'as he has loved us'. We love like him to the extent that we renounce all possessiveness and give ourselves to others, allowing them to be themselves, happy that our love has helped them become the persons God wants them to be – necessarily different from us.

The great St Augustine looked at eating the Eucharist from a different, indeed opposite, angle. He took as his starting point that when we eat food, it is changed into our bodies; he said that in the Eucharist the opposite happens: when we eat the body of Christ we are turned into his body. Both interpretations of the Eucharistic meal are true and both are found in the teaching of Jesus, 'on that day you will know that I am in my Father, and you in me and I in you' (John 14:20). Whatever way we look at it, we should pay more attention to this union between us and Jesus, symbolised and effected in the Eucharist.

I find that many people relate to Jesus in the same way both before and after Communion. In doing this we neglect the meaning of the Eucharist. I would recommend that after receiving Communion we focus on the fact that we and Jesus are one, we in him and he in us. We become conscious of him; bringing us to the Father, praying to the Father within us, and of course in himself uniting us with the whole of creation.

This is tremendously important today because of the widespread contempt for people and for the human body, which is one of the characteristics of our modern culture. Jesus challenges this contempt in a way so bold and radical that no human being could have dared think it up

– he unites his body with ours. When St Paul speaks of 'not recognising the body', he means celebrating the Eucharist with no respect for members of the community who are in need (1 Corinthians 11:17-27).

We must understand reverence for the Eucharist from this perspective. The moment that, more than any other, should fill us with 'wonder and awe' is the Communion rite – when we ourselves receive, see others receiving, or minister to them. I have been a priest for many years, but I still find myself deeply touched when I see the Communion procession coming up before me. Especially so in a parish church with its extraordinary mix of people, different social classes, older folk barely able to make it, young ones sprightly and nervy, fathers and mothers with a baby in their arms or children trailing after them.

All come up as free children of God, confident that in Jesus he wishes to unite himself with them, they are 'no longer aliens or foreign or visitors but citizens like all the saints' (Ephesians 2:19).

I find, by the way, that receiving communion in the hand is particularly touching and must confess myself bewildered that anyone would see it as less reverent than receiving it on the tongue. Jesus literally entrusts himself into our hands. We think of how poor people are treated in our society, in offices and public institutions, yet here they are taking the body of Christ into their own hands. I imagine the choirs of angels gathering around in awe at the sight and singing, 'Holy, holy, holy is the Lord'.

In this, as in many other ways, the Eucharist, like Jesus himself, challenges our entire value system and sends us out to build a different kind of world. In countries where there was official racial discrimination, such as in the Southern States of America, or South Africa under apartheid, Churches too were segregated. It was a terrible negation of all that Jesus stood for, but at least there was some logic in what they were doing. The Eucharist is a sign of unity, so it makes no sense celebrating with people you look down on or do not want to associate with. The terrible spectable of a segregated Eucharist is, in a perverse way, the logical consequence of a segregated lifestyle. The Eucharist, especially at the Communion rite, attacks all forms of discrimination at the root: God gives himself to all to be eaten and drunk.

The way this message is conveyed is very significant. Our culture believes that to make ourselves heard we must be loud, aggressive, combative. The Eucharist, like all the sacraments, teaches powerfully but as sacrament, without words or noise of any kind, purely by the silent, non-violent language of its symbolism.

The ideas I have tried to express here are summed up in the Post-Communion Prayer of the Seventh Sunday of Ordinary Time:

> Almighty God,
> help us to live the example of love we celebrate in this Eucharist,
> that we may come to its fulfilment in your presence.

2

FRUIT OF THE EARTH AND WORK OF HUMAN HANDS

At every Mass the priest says the following blessing prayer over the offering of bread:

> Blessed are you, Lord, God of all creation.
> Through your goodness we have this bread to offer,
> Which earth has given and human hands have made.
> It will become for us the bread of life.

This prayer was introduced into the rite of the Mass after the Second Vatican Council. It is said by the priest alone, usually in low tones while the offertory hymn is being sung, so that it is not heard by the congregation. This is unfortunate because it is a very deep and beautiful prayer and can help us understand the Eucharist better. We need to reflect on it and pray it personally.

What is transformed into the body of Christ, the prayer reminds us, is 'fruit of the earth and work of human hands'.

This is an aspect of the Eucharist that our Church has tended to neglect in recent centuries. In fact, the tendency has been to play it down. In our Church, 'altar bread', as we call it, is prepared in such a way that it does not resemble ordinary bread. It looks and feels different, is usually baked by a religious community, and kept in a special container and a special place in the sacristy.

Up to quite recently, we were taught not to receive Holy Communion as if we were eating bread. We spoke of 'consuming' the sacred host and allowing it to touch the teeth was considered a lack of reverence, even sinful.

Nowadays, the Church invites us to have a different attitude. We must not merely accept, but celebrate ('bless God'), that Jesus comes to us in the form of bread, and that this bread is the 'work of human hands'.

To bring home the point, let us remember a time when we turned up for Mass and found there was no bread. The congregation was there, the priest was there, prayers were being said, hymns sung, holy people were offering themselves to God, but none of that made any difference. All had to wait until someone brought the bread.

This experience reminds us of something we don't usually advert to, but is actually very extraordinary if we think about it. For us to be able to celebrate the Eucharist we need others; God leaves us, indeed leaves himself, at the mercy of others.

These 'others' seem at first to be one or two people associated with the church – the sexton who has the key to the sacristy, the driver bringing the bread from a neighbouring parish. In fact, however, we depend on many others, those who plant and reap the wheat, those who turn it into flour, those who transport it to the convent for baking.

Most of them are unconnected to us, may not even have faith in Jesus, but we are dependent on every one of them. If even one link in the chain does not function we cannot have the Eucharist.

God put himself in this predicament – if we want to call it that – by design. It is the logic of the incarnation. God's normal way of coming into the world is now through people, the Word has become flesh.

The many people, therefore, who make it possible for Jesus to be present in the Eucharist symbolise the very many more who make it possible for us to experience God in our daily lives.

They include not merely family, friends and neighbours, but all the people who have inspired us, our role-models, those who built our civilisation, indeed the whole human family, since each person is a unique reflection of the face of God. God's presence in the world is always 'work of human hands' and the Eucharist is the 'sacrament' of that.

When in the first chapter of his gospel St Matthew tells us 'how Jesus Christ came to be born', he starts the story way back with Abraham, tracing the genealogy of Jesus. The list is long and includes some very disreputable characters. Among them, the series of kings of whom the Book of Ecclesiasticus says, 'Apart from David, Hezekiah and Josiah, they all heaped wrong on wrong, since they disregard the Law of the Most High, since they gave their strength to others and their honour to a foreign nation' (Ecclesiastes 49:4-6). St Matthew is reminding us that we must celebrate them all, because they are all part of the story of Jesus.

The blessing prayer invites us to do the same as we approach the Eucharistic Prayer, to enter into communion not merely with Jesus as a single person but with his entire body, the Church.

In him we are united with all those whose 'human hands' have made this moment possible, those who have gone before us 'whose faith is known to [God] alone' (Fourth Eucharistic Prayer), and also the living '[God's] children wherever they may be,' (Third Eucharistic Prayer).

The blessing prayer invites us to widen our horizons further; the bread before us is also 'fruit of the earth'. Without the earth there can be no Eucharist for us to celebrate.

This earth too, of which the bread before us is the fruit, has a history. It is the climax of a long evolutionary process lasting millions of years, it has had to survive many natural disasters and be tilled by generations of farmers, so that it could produce the wheat that would become the bread that is now on the altar.

Just as with the 'human hands', every link in that long chain was necessary for us to celebrate the Eucharist. The blessing prayer invites us to be aware of this, to enter into humble, respectful communion with the earth.

Doing this is very important today. The earth, God's beautiful earth, is being destroyed because human beings don't respect it and consider it a thing, a commodity to be bartered, used for what it can produce and then thrown away.

Sad to say, we Christians too have contributed to this lack of respect, and one of the reasons is that we have not reflected on the Eucharist as 'fruit of the earth'.

The Eucharist is a living lesson of the great mystery, which St Paul taught us, that the whole of creation is the body of Christ. He is, as St Paul says in the Epistle to the Colossians, 'the first born of all creation, in him were created all things in heaven and earth, everything visible and everything invisible, all things were created through him and for him.'

The small amount of bread on the altar, about to be transformed into the body of Christ, is a symbol of the whole universe created 'for him'. We who are present in the church are privileged to be in communion with that glorious transformation.

As we accustom ourselves – and teach the young ones at First Communion – to be aware of these dimensions of the Eucharist, we will quite naturally begin to see the world differently – with eyes of faith.

We will see nature as God's handiwork, destined as St Paul says 'to enjoy the same freedom and glory as the children of God' (Romans 8:21). Through our work in our different vocations, we are the 'human hands' that in God's plan bring his work of creation to its fruition.

The world is no longer a hostile place, but the dwelling place of God. It becomes for us the bread of life. Then we can truly say, 'Blessed are you, Lord, God of all creation.'

3

BREAD TO BE EATEN

Jesus makes himself present among us in the form of bread to be eaten. What does this teach us about our relationship with him?

When we eat something we take a risk. To bring this out, we can remember a time when a strange dish was put before us at table, when we came across a strange fruit as we walked in the forest, or we had to take a new medicine. We looked suspiciously at it, wondered what it would taste like; if it was good for us, would we keep it down? We know instinctively that when we eat something we give ourselves to it and must take the consequences.

The Eucharist is telling us that our relationship with Jesus is like that, we must give ourselves to him and there are consequences for us. He won't make a difference to our lives if we hold back and make only a partial commitment – 'Don't go overboard', 'You can't take what he says literally', 'You have to be practical', 'Give me some time to make up my mind', 'On the one hand ... on the other hand'.

Jesus himself said, 'Unless you eat the flesh of the Son of Man and drink of his blood, you shall not have life in you.' The Eucharist says the same thing: for Jesus to give life to us, we must take the risk of eating him.

We find the symbol of eating in several books of the Bible. When the prophet Ezekiel was given a word to preach, he was told, 'Open your mouth and eat what I am about to give you'; he was then given the prophetic scroll and told, 'Eat and be satisfied by the scroll I am giving you' (Ezekiel 3:1-3). In the Book of Revelation too, St John was given a scroll and told, 'Take it and eat it' (Revelation 10:9).

We should remember these texts when we go to Communion and the minister shows us the Sacred Host. Our 'amen' is saying: 'I will not be content with a partial commitment to Jesus, I want to take the risk of eating him.'

Dieticians often say, 'We are what we eat'. Eating is a risk because it is not simply a transfer of nourishment, we become physically one with the food, it enters our bloodstream. In the Eucharist too we 'become what we eat', and that is Jesus, offering himself.

This is the constant teaching of the New Testament, and especially of St Paul. It is not sufficient to say that we are believers in Jesus' message or his imitators, our relationship with him is physical, he enters into our bloodstream, we are 'in Christ', 'his body'.

St John's gospel, too, speaks of a physical relationship. At the Last Supper for example, Jesus said to the apostles, 'on that day you will learn that you are in me and I am in you'.

This aspect of the Eucharist is very important for us today. In so many ways our modern world degrades the human body, which in St Paul's dramatic phrase, 'belongs to Christ'.

We think of the countless victims of torture, of domestic violence, of malnutrition, or bad health care, those who use the body – theirs or another's – only for pleasure. The body is so often an object of scorn, people are looked down on because of their physical features – they belong to a certain race, are deformed, or simply do not conform to social norms.

By becoming physically one with Jesus in the Eucharist we are entering into the truth that the human body is holy, offered in sacrifice in union with his sacrifice on Calvary, a fragrant offering in the presence of the Father. This is true, not only of ourselves, but of every person in the whole world. To disrespect the human body is to disrespect what Jesus has taken to himself and offered to the Father.

'Becoming Jesus' means becoming his entire body, and this is, at a first level, our brothers and sisters in the Church. Through the Eucharist we experience that we form one body with them, according to Jesus' prayer to the Father at the Last Supper, 'May they all be one, Father, as you are in me and I am in you.'

With today's modern means of communication, we are aware of what is happening in our Church in other parts of the world. Often the stories are sad, for example the Church suffering persecution because leaders are protesting against injustice, being disfigured by violent conflicts between different factions, or humiliated by scandals among the clergy. Sometimes, on the contrary, it is a glorious story of heroic deeds or deep prayer.

At the Eucharist we experience that we are part of both, carrying in our hearts to the Father the pains and the joys of the Church.

It is not merely our brothers and sisters in the Church that we are in union with at the Eucharist, but the whole of creation. According to the teaching of St Paul, Jesus 'holds all things in unity' (Colossians 1:17); at the Eucharist we experience that we are part of this 'unity', one with nature and with the human family.

At the Eucharist especially, we can say with the Second Vatican Council that 'the joys and the hopes, the griefs and the anxieties of men and women today, especially those who are poor or are in any way afflicted, these are our joys and hopes, griefs and anxieties.'

The body of Christ that we 'become' at the Eucharist is his risen, glorious body. The Eucharist is therefore a foretaste of the future, when we, the whole of humanity and the earth itself will be transformed into the glorious body of Christ. At the Eucharist, we anticipate the glorious moment described in the Apocalypse when 'voices can be heard shouting in heaven, calling, "The kingdom of this world has become the kingdom of our Lord and his Christ, and he will reign for ever and ever"' (Revelation 11:15).

That, however, is the future. The Eucharist also situates us in the present when we have not 'become' but are 'becoming' Christ, growing, as St Paul says, 'in all ways into Christ ... until we become the perfect Man, fully mature with the fullness of Christ himself' (Ephesians 4:13,15).

Interestingly, the Eucharistic Prayers draw a parallel between the bread and wine 'becoming Christ' and the community (the people gathered in the church, representing the whole of humanity) also 'becoming Christ'.

In the third prayer, for example, the priest prays before the words of consecration, that the 'power of the Holy Spirit' will come upon the bread and wine so that 'it may become the body and blood of Christ'; after the consecration he prays, 'that we who are nourished by his body and blood may be filled with his Holy Spirit and become one body, one spirit in Christ.'

So too we pray in the fourth prayer, 'By your Holy Spirit, gather all who share in this one bread and one cup into the one body of Christ, a living sacrifice of praise.'

EUCHARIST AS WORD

This is only a comparison, of course. There is a big difference between the two 'becomings'. Whereas we keep our identities, the bread and wine are totally changed into the body and blood of Christ; after the consecration only Christ is present, not bread and wine.

We can however celebrate our own 'becoming'. The Eucharist invites us to enter gratefully into the little victories of grace in the world – enemies reconciled, exiles welcomed home, hungry people fed and the naked clothed – what Pope Paul VI called 'the world which, in spite of its ignorance, its mistakes and even its sins, its relapses into barbarism and its wanderings far from the road to salvation is, even unawares, taking slow but sure steps towards its Creator' (*Populorum progressio*, No. 79).

The Eucharist is truly the source and summit of the Christian life; let us celebrate this mystery of faith. One conclusion we can draw is that after Communion is not really an appropriate time for saying prayers – making promises or asking favours. What we should focus on doing at this most sacred of all moments is simply to rest in Jesus, allowing him to gather us into his body.

4

EUCHARIST AS SELF-GIVING

Let us explore further why Jesus gave himself to us in the form of bread to be eaten.

As we have seen, there is a sense in which we can say that we 'become what we eat'. In fact the opposite is correct – what we eat becomes us.

Food nourishes us, but does not change our appearance. When we have finished a meal, the food that was on the plate is nowhere to be found, but it has not disappeared; through the process of assimilation, it has been transformed into us.

Something similar happens in the Eucharist. When we look around the Church after Communion we do not see Jesus, all we see is one another; we can say that he has been transformed into us.

Here is another very deep, living, lesson of how Jesus relates with us. He comes to nourish us spiritually, to take us out of our sinful ways and to make us more like himself, but he does all this without taking away our individuality. Like food, he nourishes us by entering humbly into our unique way of being in the world.

God has given each of us a name, entrusted to us a place in human history that he has given to no one else who has ever lived or will ever live. We relate with God by entering freely and joyfully into our personal vocation.

By giving himself to us as a piece of bread to be eaten, Jesus is telling us, 'I want to be at the heart of your life but not to make you different from the unique person my Father has called you to be. I want my presence with you to be such that someone looking at you would not notice me at all, but would see only you, answering to your own name'.

This is, of course, very different from the sinful ways of the world. We have all had experience of people – relatives, teachers, spiritual guides, friends – who tried to make us into little carbon copies of themselves. We have seen groups (including Church groups) where everybody speaks, dresses, and even walks like the leader.

The dominating, oppressive way in which authority is exercised in the world is totally different from Jesus' divine way, selfless, humble, discreet, unobstrusive – just like bread.

Jesus came into the world to give abundant life, and one of the sure signs of life is that there is creativity and infinite variety, people constantly surprised by new things emerging in unexpected ways and places.

Jesus' presence in the world after his resurrection and ascension into heaven is so hidden that, in his own words at the Last Supper, it is visible only to people of faith and not to 'the world' (John 14:17). St Mark's gospel ends by making the same point: 'At the right hand of God he took his place, while they going out, preached everywhere, the Lord working with them and confirming the word by the signs that accompanied it' (Mark 16:19-20).

We in the Caribbean sing a hymn by Fr Clyde Harvey called 'To Be the Body'. In it Jesus says, 'No eyes have I, no ears to hear, you must be my body and have a father's care'.

Understanding this way of Jesus is very important for healthy spiritual growth. We spend a lot of energy trying to be who we are not called to be, or resenting that we are not like others.

Modern media reinforce this error, mainly through advertising and the soap operas. We are constantly being bombarded with images of role models that make us feel that the way we are is not good enough. We must admit that some ways of presenting the message of Jesus err in this direction too. Moralising sermons, misguided spiritual guidance, can alienate rather than be the good news of Jesus' liberation.

The Eucharist teaches us the true way of conversion. Sin, correctly understood, is always a betrayal of the truth of ourselves; conversion is returning to this truth. We cannot therefore bring others (or ourselves for that matter) to conversion by violence. On the contrary we must walk with them (and with ourselves), very discreetly, on tip-toe as it were, so careful must we be not to impose ourselves on them.

Like Jesus in the Eucharist, we must make our home in others so that they can learn to be at home with themselves. It is an application of his teaching, 'Love one another as I have loved you'. John the Baptist is our model when he says, 'There stands among you, unknown to you, the one who is coming after me and I am not fit to undo the strap of his sandals.'

This is also how the Church must integrate itself into various cultures, a big issue in our time when it is becoming indigenous in parts of the world where up to now it was present as a foreign element. The Eucharist teaches us Jesus' way of being a transforming presence, through which the culture keeps its identity and becomes the best that it can be.

People today sometimes look back with regret to the time when the Eucharist was the same everywhere. No matter what country of the world you went to, you knew that you would find Mass being celebrated in the same Latin language, with the same prayers and chants, and, to a certain extent, the same kind of sermon.

It was a very comforting thing, but a form of worship that had emerged in Europe was being imposed on the rest of the world. The problem was that Jesus' simple rite of breaking bread had become complicated and therefore culturally limited.

One of the reforms of the Council was to simplify the rites, so that the Eucharist could once more be easily adapted to various cultures, and we could experience St Paul's teaching, that 'we though many form one body because we partake of the one bread' (1 Corinthians 10:17).

Jesus' respect for the diversity of his Father's creatures extends to nature and this, too, he teaches us in the Eucharist. We need to reflect on how in God's plan, by the process that we call transubstantiation, the bread and wine are changed into the body and blood of Jesus, and yet keep their appearances.

Some Christians do not accept that there is a real substantial change and, though our own faith as Catholics tells us differently, we can understand why they think the way they do; the bread and wine look exactly as they did before. This brings out how God respects his creation, the work of his hands, a much needed lesson today, when we think that we have the right to disfigure nature for the sake of human development.

The Eucharist teaches us that even the final establishment of God's kingdom will not be a destruction, but a transformation of nature. 'The will of him who sent me is that I should lose nothing of all he has given to me, but that I should raise it up at the last day' (John 6:39).

5

PROCLAIMING HIS DEATH

'Every time you eat this bread and drink this cup, you are proclaiming his death' (1 Corinthians 11:26).

The *Catechism of the Catholic Church* has reiterated our traditional teaching that the Eucharist is a true sacrifice because it 're-presents (makes present) the sacrifice of the cross, is its memorial and applies its fruit' (No. 1366).

The Eucharistic signs of 'eating the bread and drinking the cup' can help us experience the 'memorial' or, as St Paul says, the 'proclamation' of the death of Jesus.

Our Church has always understood that the death of Jesus on the cross has many aspects, and needs to be approached from different angles.

In the New Testament writings, the early Christians used a variety of biblical symbols to explain it. It was the passover lamb slain (1 Corinthians 5:7), the suffering servant healing others by his wounds (1 Peter 2:24), the High Priest entering the Holy of Holies sprinkled with his own blood (Hebrews 9:12), the new Adam restoring by his obedience what the first one lost by his disobedience (Romans 5:19).

Jesus himself used biblical symbols to prepare his disciples to understand Calvary. For example, he reminded them of how Moses lifted up the serpent in the wilderness, and concluded: 'When you have lifted up the Son of Man you will know that I am He' (John 8:28).

The washing of the disciples' feet at the Last Supper was that kind of preparation too: 'At the moment, you do not understand what I am doing, but later you will understand,' he told them (John 13:7). He was saying, in effect, 'When tomorrow you see me dying on the cross you will be very confused, and wonder what it means. At that moment ('later' in the text), my washing of your feet will help you understand that on the cross I humbled myself so that you could be made clean.'

In a similar way, he gave us the Eucharist as a teaching on the mystery of the cross. When we eat bread, we can say that it is 'sacrificed'; it loses its identity – not as a negative movement, but a life-giving one, through which we who eat it become healthy and energetic. This is a touching metaphor of what happened on Calvary. Jesus 'became bread', in that he gave himself so that we might live.

He used a similar metaphor during the final days of his ministry in Jerusalem before his passion: 'Unless a wheat grain falls into the earth and dies, it remains only a single grain; but if it dies it yields a rich harvest' (John 12:24). Bread remaining on the table is safe, looks attractive perhaps, but it is not life-giving, it becomes so only if it 'dies' and becomes nourishing food.

As in all his parables, Jesus is articulating a universal truth, a law of life. Death on a cross, as 'proclaimed' in the Eucharist, is the process that all 'life-givers' must go through.

The Eucharist celebrates, therefore, not merely Jesus giving himself on the cross, but also 'through him, with him and in him', all those who give themselves like bread, so that others might live – the multitude of parents, friends, teachers, nurses and doctors, Church ministers who are 'eaten up' by others and become a source of life for them.

It celebrates great people of the past too, those who gave their lives so that people of every race could be accepted as equal, that women would be respected, children protected, the elderly cared for.

St Paul speaks of 'proclaiming' this life-giving death, and indeed, we need to be loud and clear about it, because it goes against the dominant value-system of our culture. One of the basic tenets of modern Western culture is that we must look after ourselves first, and share with others only what we have left over.

Nowadays, people are afraid of giving themselves. We tend to think that we can be spouse, parent, friend, leader of a noble enterprise, by a part-time commitment, holding something back, protecting ourselves from being eaten up; 'It must be fifty-fifty,' we say.

Experience teaches us that this just doesn't work for our deep relationships. We cannot be life-giving except if we give our flesh as food and our blood as drink. This is what we learn from Jesus on Calvary – and the mystery of bread that is eaten – 'Having loved those who were his in the world, [he] loved them to the end' (John 13:1).

Of course, we must understand self-giving correctly. To die is always a terrifying prospect. It is a value only if it brings new life into the world, to ourselves and to others. If we give ourselves with resentment or self-pity or measuring the cost, then we will not be life-giving.

What happens at the Eucharist can serve as a model. After Mass, people stand around, chatting, laughing, making plans for the day – as people do after a good meal, or like children who enjoy themselves, knowing that this makes their parents happy too. Christ has died, has risen and has come again.

We often have to experience this bread-like, life-giving dying within our own selves too. As we go through life, we carve out an image of ourselves that we have settled for and are comfortable with; we are 'Mr or Mrs Nice', or the opposite, 'Mr or Mrs whom no one takes advantage of'; we can stand on our own two feet or we always need to be propped up by others; we are 'holy' or 'sinners'.

Then, quite unexpectedly, something happens that reveals a side to ourselves that we never suspected or, if we knew it was there, tried to conceal. We are not as meek as we thought, as self-reliant, as forgiving, or as confident.

Because of our faith in God's love, revealed to us in Jesus, we can allow that false self to die as bread dies when it is eaten, so that our true self can emerge, better in some ways than we thought and worse in other ways, but in either case more true and more alive. This is the movement of 'losing ourselves' and 'finding ourselves', which Jesus taught (for example in Mark 9:35). Jesus lived what he taught. 'He did not cling to his equality with God, but emptied himself to assume the condition of a slave' (Philippians 2:7).

Often too, life tears up great and beautiful plans we make for ourselves – perfect marriage, well-balanced children, successful career, friends we can rely on, healthy old age. We become life-giving if, in faith, we allow our plans to die and become life-giving as we allow them – like bread that is eaten – to be transformed into God's plans for us.

In this way too, Jesus has shown us the way. He wanted passionately to renew the Jewish religion by bringing it back to its original purity. To implement this plan, he started in a small way, hopefully, in a Galilean village with a group of chosen disciples.

That plan had to die, however, before the reality of his Father's will. 'He resolutely turned his face towards

Jerusalem' (Luke 9:51), knowing that he would be rejected by the religious leaders, betrayed by one of his disciples, handed over to the Romans by his own people. It was a life-giving death, by which 'he became perfect and for all who obey him the source of eternal salvation' (Hebrews 5:9).

Life-giving death is the wondrous 'mystery of our faith', which the priest invites us to proclaim at Mass after holding up the newly consecrated host.

At the moment of receiving the sacred host we go a step further in our 'proclamation', we enter into the mystery, in communion with Jesus and through him with all our brothers and sisters of the human family.

How great indeed is the mystery of our faith.

6

EUCHARIST AND MISSION

The word 'mission' comes from the Latin word 'sent'. The Church is called 'missionary' because it does not exist for itself; by its very nature, it is for others – like bread. We must insist on this because, right through the history of our Church, its members have tended to remain closed in on themselves, looking after their own needs, spiritual and material, and leaving those outside to fend for themselves.

A Church closed in on itself is not the true Church of Christ. No matter how large or how prosperous our Church community is, there are, and always will be, people outside it and we as a community must have a care for them.

The Church of the New Testament was a tiny, insignificant minority within the Roman empire, but the Christians did not isolate themselves from their fellow-citizens, they knew they had a mission to them.

It is sigificant that the Eucharist itself can become individualistic. We can (and often do) experience it as an in-house exercise, focusing on ourselves, our families and our Church community – praying for our needs and thanking God for his gifts to us.

This is contrary to the sign of bread. We do not buy bread to remain on the shelf, but to feed ourselves and others. Jesus gave himself to us under the appearance of bread to teach us that we too are for others. Eucharist is mission.

The new Eucharistic Prayers invite us to carry the world in our hearts. Prayer 3, for example, prays, 'May this sacrifice which has made our peace with you, advance the peace and salvation of all the world', and again, 'In mercy and love unite your children wherever they may be.'

Even the prayers of the dead have this wide scope. We pray not only for 'departed brothers and sisters' but for 'all who have left this world in your friendship' (Prayer 3), not merely for 'those who have died in the peace of Christ' but also for 'all the dead whose faith is known to you alone' (Prayer 4).

Knowing that we have a mission to share what we have with the wider human community raises a further issue. In the course of its long history our Church has sometimes been very unjust to the very people it felt sent to.

Pope John Paul called our attention to this fact in *Tertio Millenio Adveniente,* his letter announcing the jubilee year 2000. 'A painful chapter of history to which the sons and daughters of the Church must return with a spirit of repentance is that of the acquiescence given, especially in certain centuries, to intolerance and even the use of violence in the service of truth' (No. 35).

These errors, the Pope said, 'sullied' the face of Christ, 'prevented the Church from fully mirroring the image of our crucified Lord, the supreme witness of patient love and humble meekness.'

Nowadays we do not 'use violence in the service of truth' but there are other ways in which we can 'sully the face of Christ'.

In our modern world, many other groups see themselves as having a 'mission'. They have a way of life, a political programme, a value system or a product, which they want to 'sell' to others and have developed effective methods of doing it. They use threats for example, military or financial, the 'media blitz', bombarding people with facts and ensuring that they do not reflect critically on the message. The reality is polished up, a 'spin' put on it, so that what is on offer looks better than it is.

We can find these 'missionary methods' so effective that we are tempted to use them in our mission too. They do not, however, 'mirror the image of our crucified Lord'. If on the contrary, we see ourselves as 'bread for the world', we will naturally imitate his 'supreme witness of patient love and humble meekness'.

The linking of Eucharist and mission is not found explicitly in the New Testament, but we can take it as a logical conclusion of Jesus' teaching, 'as the Father sent me, so I am sending you'. In John 6, Jesus invites us to look on him as 'the bread of God which comes down from heaven and gives life to the world' (John 6:33). We can conclude that he sends us too, as individuals and as a Church, to be the bread of God, which gives life to our world.

We can discern three ways in which bread gives life to those whom it feeds. It is life-giving, it is humble, it operates from within.

Seeing ourselves as bread for the world tells us that the role of our Church is always to be a source of life in society. As a community, we must be against all forms of death dealing, in public policy as well as personal relationships. We must bring new ideas where there is stagnation, hope for new possibilities where people feel they have no future.

Creativity is always a sign of life and it must be a sign too of the presence of the Church. Just as bread nourishes by entering into the bloodstream and the digestive system, the Church too must enter into the life-giving processes of people and of a society.

We are like bread when we meet people and groups at the level where they are at their best, noblest, most generous and trusting. We do not foster creativity when we speak to their lack of self-worth, their need to feel superior to others or their desire for power. The key, of course, is that we too come to people from the best of ourselves, not with suspicion, fear or arrogance.

Bread is consumed by being eaten, so we are like bread when we come to the world without any great concern about our identity, whether we are acknowledged or praised. It should be normal for us that people do not notice that it was a Church person or a Church institution that began a project.

The Church introduced credit unionism into many countries, for example, and we rejoice that others have taken it over. We rejoice too that very many people of other Churches and religions receive their education in our Church schools and don't feel any pressure to join us.

We are like bread, therefore, when we influence the world from within, when members of our Church, including priests and religious, make their contribution to society in their different professions and jobs, and within non-Church institutions, distinguished only by their professionalism, vision and dedication.

Church schools and hospitals are like bread when – while remaining faithful to Jesus' life-giving values – they take their place among other similar institutions, not looking for special privileges, fighting to prove they are better or competing with others for space.

The Church must not look for spectacular or instant results. It works from the bottom up, starts small and lets things develop at their own pace, like salt, leaven, a mustard seed planted in the ground – like bread and like Jesus.

Adapting the words of Jesus, we can say that bread teaches us to be meek and humble of heart, so that those of the wider community who are heavily burdened by having to protect themselves from the many groups who want to dominate and manipulate them, will come to us and find rest for their souls.

We pray that all our Eucharistic celebrations will nourish among us a true missionary spirituality – one after the heart of Jesus, the bread of life.

7

EUCHARIST AND WORD

We pray that this Eucharist may accomplish in your Church the unity and peace it signifies.

This post-Communion prayer for the eleventh Sunday of Ordinary Time was composed many centuries ago; it is very deep and beautiful. It reminds us that the Eucharist 'signifies' something; it is a 'living lesson' as I have been showing in the previous chapters.

What the Eucharist 'signifies', according to the prayer, is 'unity and peace'. This is what it should 'accomplish' in the Church.

We must go further. The Vatican Council teaches that the Church is itself a 'sacrament' (living lesson, sign and effective instrument) of humanity or, to be more accurate, of what humanity should be. We conclude that the Eucharist 'signifies' and is meant to 'accomplish' peace and unity not merely in the Church but in every human community.

When we attend a well-executed Sunday liturgy, we should be able to say, in the words of a popular modern hymn, 'We've been to the mountain and had a glimpse of what the world could be' and feel more committed than before to turning that vision into a reality.

Following this line of thought, I invite you to imagine an outsider coming to a Sunday Mass, reflecting on the experience and drawing conclusions about the 'unity and peace' of a human community – family, work place, neighbourhood, nation, the human family as a whole.

> The first thing that struck me was how many different kinds of people made up this

community. Every race and mixture of races, every social class and every age was represented. There were babes in the arms of their parents, toddlers, teenagers, elderly people needing help to walk. Some arrived on foot, some in fancy cars; a couple of vagrants sat in the back or stood outside.

Yet we formed a community; everyone was involved in what was happening to everyone else. We had no option, even those who tried to concentrate on their own prayers. A baby cried and we looked around, we smiled at a little girl who strayed away from her parents, looked suspiciously at a strange character who walked boldly up the centre aisle to the front of the Church, crossed himself and walked back down.

I thought that this was our family, work place, neighbourhood, the human family. We are very different from one another, and yet God has called us to share the same limited space; what any of us does impacts on all the others.

The next thing I noticed was how people were assigned different functions and how dependent we were on the way that they carried out their functions – just as in every community. The day I was there, the reader of the first reading was not very good and we had no idea what the author wanted to communicate. The reader of the second reading was excellent, and the deep words spoke to our hearts.

The acolytes delayed bringing up the gifts, and there wasn't a thing the priest or any of us could do about it. Like the rest of us, he just had to wait. The thought crossed my mind that God himself had to wait for them before he could work the conversion of bread and wine. What an example of human relations he gives us here!

We depended on the choir especially; they made the difference as to whether we felt in the presence of God or not. Isn't that how community is too? Through the harmony (or cacophony) of our lives, we can help (or prevent) one another to experience God's presence.

Early in the service we confessed – to God, to one another and to the angels and saints – that we were sinners. To me, it was significant that we started that way. The foundation of our being a community, what keeps us united, is not how great, but how honest we are, the fact that we need one another's forgiveness and prayers.

Another thing that made us a community was that we were all subject to a higher authority – the authority of God. In this regard, the physical arrangement of the sanctuary was significant. Even though the priest's chair was more ornate than those of the other ministers, it was not in the centre. The altar was in the central place – a reminder (sacrament) that we don't call any man 'father' because we have only one Father and he is in heaven. Catholics do call their priests 'Father', but not in the sense rejected by Jesus – at least they shouldn't.

We got the same message when the Bible was being read. We all listened – including the priest. After the elevation first of the host and then of the cup, he invited us to bow low with him. I heard afterward that this is not the official rite, but perhaps it should be. At least, I found it very touching.

I thought how every community needs to have times when everybody listens respectfully – a child tells the story of what happened at school, someone finally gets around to saying how hurt they are, to confessing some fault or asking for help, a neighbour in distress visits. There are other times when a community should simply keep silent, wonder at the beauty of nature, of love, fidelity, togetherness – these things too are words of God.

It was an orderly community. There were ushers to ensure that we filled up empty seats but without overcrowding. The various processions were well organised and done with great courtesy, even the one for Holy Communion, which included most of the people present – there was a lot of making way for one another.

This was also (I should really say 'therefore') a community that knew how to be spontaneous. Every once in a way everyone would break into hand-clapping and rhythmic movements. The sign of peace especially was spontaneous and beautifully disorganised, some remaining in their places and giving a cold handshake, others full of exuberance but rather superficial; of course, the children had a great time running around. It reminded me of the neighbourhood parties that have become popular at Christmas and at carnival and bring people together who up to then were strangers.

I thought too how a good community can keep a balance between order and spontaneity. Without order, spontaneity quickly becomes destructive, but order can easily become oppressive. The powerful make all the decisions and the humble ones become marginalised.

This was not a community that remained turned in on itself. They prayed, not merely for their own needs, but for the whole nation and also for far away countries like Albania, Sri Lanka and Israel. How true to life this was! Wherever human beings are suffering, we are affected somehow. I noticed, however, that they were careful not to be self-righteous. They prayed for God's children 'wherever they may be' and when they prayed for the dead, added 'whose faith is known to you alone'. If only our various human communities could be similarly non-judgemental!

This community reverenced nature, since the highlight of the ceremony was bread and wine becoming the body and blood of Christ. The priest took the trouble to remind us that the bread and wine had not come down directly from heaven, but was the 'fruit of the earth and work of human hands'. How different a world we would live in, if we could always keep before our minds that we are dependent on the earth and the work of human hands.

I remember reading, in a text from one of St Paul's epistles, that the whole of creation is destined to share in the glorious destiny of humanity. 'The Eucharist makes the same promise,' I thought. We would certainly have more reverence for the soil, the trees, and animals if we kept that in mind.

Lord we pray that this Eucharist may truly accomplish in all our human communities the unity and peace it signifies.

PART II

INTRODUCTION

The biblical meditations in this section follow the ancient method of bible reading called *lectio divina*. What characterises *lectio divina*, making it different from other methods of bible reading, is that the biblical text is at its centre. *Lectio divina* starts and ends with the reading of the text, done in three stages:

1. *Lectio* during which the text is read in its entirety, slowly and reverentially.

2. *Meditatio* during which we recognise our experience in the text; we remember events
   - in our personal lives
   - in the lives of people who touched us, people near to us or on the world stage
   - in the lives of our communities, our Church, local community, nation, the human family
   - in nature.

   Every bible text is simultaneously a story of grace and a story of sin, and through meditation we recognise both stories.

3. *Oratio*. Meditation leads spontaneously to prayer, expressed in three registers:
   - Thanksgiving, flowing from the story of grace that we have recognised
   - Humility, flowing from the story of sin
   - Petition, flowing from our consciousness that there is room for a greater manifestation of grace. Every petition says in one form or another, 'Come Lord Jesus'.

In *lectio divina*, the prayers are expressed as far as possible in the actual words of the text, thus they become the climax, as well as the starting point, of the exercise. We find ourselves 'carried' by the text which means, of course, carried by the Word and eventually by the Lord.

The biblical story of sin and grace is universal; it is fulfilled
• in every person
• in every human community
• in the movements of nature.

Through *lectio divina*, then, we enter into communion with the story of humanity celebrating its graces, lamenting its sins, feeling its potential to rise above the limitations of the present. We also enter into communion with nature, which St Paul reminds us, is also 'groaning in the one great act of giving birth' (Romans 8:22).

We are lifted up by this communion. Humanity's great stories of grace – the lives of the saints, past and present – become our family stories. We are also humbled as we become aware of our communion with humanity's sins, those of past ages and of our times. This communion affects our petitions too, as they express humanity's deepest aspirations, here again those of all ages and those of our particular time.

Each meditation in this section of the book comprises three sections, corresponding to the three stages of *lectio divina:*
• The section of John 6 being proposed for meditation
• A meditation on the text

- A series of prayers flowing from the meditation. These move between the three registers of thanksgiving, humility and petition and cover different areas of human life.

Several of the prayers are preceded by a quotation from one of the world's sages; this brings out how *lectio divina* is a communion with the wisdom of humanity – its true wisdom, not its false wisdom of individualism, materialism and consumerism.

JESUS, THE BREAD OF LIFE
MEDITATING ON JOHN, CHAPTER 6

John 6:1-15

¹Jesus went off to the other side of the Sea of Galilee – or of
Tiberias – ²and a large crowd followed him, impressed by the
signs he had done in curing the sick. ³Jesus climbed the hillside
and sat down there with his disciples. ⁴The time of the Jewish
Passover was near.

⁵Looking up, Jesus saw the crowds approaching and said to
Philip, 'Where can we buy some bread for these people to eat?'
⁶He said this only to put Philip to the test; he himself knew
exactly what he was going to do. ⁷Philip answered, 'Two
hundred denarii would not buy enough to give them a little piece
each.' ⁸One of his disciples, Andrew, Simon Peter's brother, said,
⁹'Here is a small boy with five barley loaves and two fish; but
what is that among so many?' ¹⁰Jesus said to them, 'Make the
people sit down,' There was plenty of grass there, and as many
as five thousand men sat down. ¹¹Then Jesus took the loaves,
gave thanks, and distributed them to those who were sitting
there; he then did the same with the fish, distributing as much
as they wanted. ¹²When they had eaten enough he said to the
disciples, 'Pick up the pieces left over, so that nothing is wasted.'
¹³So they picked them up and filled twelve large baskets with
scraps left over from the meal of five barley loaves. ¹⁴Seeing the
sign that he had done, the people said, 'This is indeed the
prophet who is to come into the world.' ¹⁵Jesus, as he realised
they were about to come and take him by force and make him
king, fled back to the hills alone.

This famous chapter, which presents Jesus as the Bread
of Life, starts with the story of the miraculous feeding
of the people by Jesus. Take the story very slowly,
watching how it unfolds and stopping at whatever
point you find touches you. It can be divided up into
sections:

- *Verses 1-3:* The stage is set; Jesus takes up his position on the other side of the sea, sitting on the hillside with his disciples. He clearly lets the people come to him on their own accord.

- *Verses 4-9:* Jesus leads the apostles on a journey of faith.

- *Verses 10-12:* The miracle of the feeding.

- *Verse 13:* The command to pick up the scraps, which has its own deep symbolism.

- *Verses 14-15:* The confrontation between Jesus and the people.

Right through the story you will find yourself identifying either with Jesus or with the people. Jesus is the great leader and teacher, the people are symbolic of ourselves being led to experience grace in a deep way, with the blessing that this implies and also the wrong responses that we easily fall into.

The dialogue between Jesus and the apostles is also very significant so you might want to focus on that aspect of the story.

Gospel Prayers

LORD, we thank you for leading us to a deeper relationship with you:
- we joined a prayer group or a religious community
- we gave up a relationship that had been harming us for many years

- we returned to confession and the Eucharist after a long break.

It was a journey you led us on, as you led the people in the wilderness. It began when we were impressed by the signs you gave in curing the sick; several people we knew had turned to you and found new meaning to their lives.
For a time, we were just following, not sure where we were going to end up; others were worrying about how we would satisfy our needs, but you knew exactly what you were going to do.
Then came the great moment of grace: we felt that you had given us all the nourishment we wanted; in fact we had enough to fill countless hampers with the left-overs. Thank you, Lord.

LORD, we pray for parents who see their children following Jesus into new places; naturally, they are concerned, worrying about where the children will get bread to eat, how they will make a living, or raise their families, or enjoy their recreation. But you are letting them feel this concern only to test them; you know exactly what you are going to do for the children.

LORD, often leaders don't believe in their people. They think the problem is finding money to buy bread for them and, of course, there is never enough even to give them a small piece each.
If only they would seek out the little people with five barley loaves and two fish, take the loaves and give thanks and give them out to all who are sitting ready, and then do the same with the fish, giving out as much as is

wanted; they will find that all will have enough and they will even pick up left-over scraps to fill twelve hampers.

One act is required, and that is all. For this one act pulls everything together and keeps everything in order. This one act is to stand with attention in your heart.
Theophane the Recluse

LORD, we thank you for our parents, teachers, those who have guided us. They allowed us to come to them of our own free will, like Jesus sitting on the hillside with his disciples. They tested us, as Jesus tested Philip when he knew exactly what he was going to do, and they waited for us to see the way forward as Jesus waited for Andrew to point out the little boy with the five barley loaves and the two fish.

LORD, the sign that we receive food as a gift from you is that we pick up the pieces left over, so that nothing gets wasted.
We thank you for those who taught us this deep truth.

We have no vision, no models or metaphors to live by. Only the saints and mystics live well in a time like this.
Denys Arcand, Canadian film director

LORD, when people impress us, immediately we see the signs they have given, we say, 'This is the prophet who is to come into the world,' and we want to take them by force and make them king.
But they always escape from our grasp. If we had experienced you, we would know that you are the only king and we cannot possess you.

Someone who knows his own weakness is greater than someone who sees the angels.
Isaac of Nineveh, Syrian monk of the 7th century

LORD, it is so important that we who are in authority or who have power over others develop our inner life; that, like Jesus, we know how to leave people and go to the other side, and there climb a hillside to be alone with our companions. Then we will have inner freedom so that when people come to take us by force and make us what we cannot be, we will be able to escape back to the hills by ourselves.

🜲 🜲 🜲 🜲 🜲

John 6:24-35

²⁴When the people saw that neither Jesus nor his disciples were there, they got into those boats and crossed to Capernaum to look for Jesus. ²⁵When they found him on the other side, they said to him, 'Rabbi, when did you come here?' ²⁶Jesus answered:

> In all truth I tell you,
> you are looking for me
> not because you have seen the signs
> but because you had all the bread
>   you wanted to eat.
> ²⁷Do not work for food that goes bad,
> but work for food
>   that endures for eternal life,
> which the Son of man will give you,
> for on him the Father, God himself,
>   has set his seal.

²⁸Then they said to him, 'What must we do if we are to carry out God's work?' ²⁹Jesus gave them this answer, 'This is carrying out God's work: you must believe in the one he has sent.' ³⁰So they said, 'What sign will you yourself do, the sight of which will make us believe in you? What work will you do? ³¹Our fathers ate manna in the desert; as scripture says: *He gave them bread from heaven to eat.*' ³²Jesus answered them:

In all truth I tell you,
it was not Moses
    who gave you the bread from heaven,
the true bread;
[33]for the bread of God
is the bread
    which comes down from heaven
and gives life to the world.

[34]'Sir,' they said, 'give us that bread always.'
[35]Jesus answered them:

I am the bread of life.
No one who comes to me will ever hunger;
no one who believes in me will ever thirst.

With this Gospel, we begin the series of teachings of Jesus which draw lessons from the miraculous feeding, all under the general theme of Jesus as Bread of Life.

As I said before, the language in these passages comes across as vague and abstract, and we must make a special effort to let them speak to our experience as all gospel passages are meant to do.

Apart from the suggestion I made above of referring back to the story of the feeding to see the teaching fulfiled practically there, it is also important to understand the biblical language as being true to our life experience.

For example, the expression 'seeing the signs', in verse 26, is the process by which we go beyond some event and discover that it tells us about life, a person, the movements of sin and grace and so on.

It is the same process that Pope John XXIII called 'interpreting the signs of the times', when he urged us to understand the significance of modern social and political movements for the gospel message.

So too, God 'sets his seal' on a person (verse 27) means that he is acting within that person, using the person as his instrument.

The expression 'eternal life', which occurs in verse 27 and several times in later passages tends, especially, to remain abstract. People often take it to mean merely 'the next life' and it does include that, but it means more.

The best approach is not to try and understand it all at once but to enter gradually into what it means. Think, for example, of deeply spiritual people, the kind of people that neither sickness nor failure nor death itself can stop from living creatively: they are living 'eternal life'.

Or you might remember a time when you felt so close to God that you felt you could face anything: that too is an experience of 'eternal life'. By referring back to experiences like these you will be touched by the teaching of Jesus.

Today's teaching takes the form of spiritual journeys that Jesus leads the people to take. We can identify three:

- *Verses 24 to 27:* Jesus leads them to move from looking to him for material food to looking for something more spiritual. You can interpret that at many different levels, our relationship with God, for example, or with one another or with some movement that we have joined

- *Verses 28 to 33:* Jesus invites the people to give up all forms of human security and put their trust in God alone. In verses 28 and 29 they are looking for the security that comes from knowing that they are doing 'the right thing'. In verses 30 and 31 it is the security of pointing to favours received or of having great leaders like Moses

- *Verses 34 and 35:* the people express good desires, but they are looking for the miraculous bread in some vague place. Jesus brings them back to reality: this bread is present in his own person.

Gospel Prayers

LORD, true friendship is a journey into a deeper kind of living, like the journey Jesus invited the people to make with him.

When we first love someone, we are all excited about it; we want to be with our newly-found friend all the time. 'When did you come here?' we are always asking.

We are still at the stage of satisfying some need of ours, working for food that cannot last.

Gradually, we realise that there is something sacred about this relationship, that you have set your seal on it and it is offering us an opportunity to live at a deeper level than we have done.

We still have a way to go: we want to do many things to please our friend, when it isn't a matter of doing anything, but of trusting.

So, too, we must stop looking for signs that we are loved, 'the kind of signs that others have got', and just keep on being grateful for this person whom you have sent to us.

Truly, such a relationship calms our restlessness and gives life.

LORD, when people come to us asking what they must do if they are to do the work you want, it is tempting to give them easy answers, 'Do this and do that, and you will be doing what God wants'.

But you want us to be honest, like Jesus, saying clearly that there is no such security for us, that the 'work' we have to do is to give ourselves to the present moment, as your gift coming down from heaven, and this is the only thing that will set us free from the hungers and thirsts which keep us in bondage.

This is the meaning of incarnation.

LORD, forgive us that we become complacent when people flock around us. Give us the wisdom of Jesus to see that:

- children come to our schools, but it is to be successful in their examinations
- people vote for us at election time because we have got them favours
- we are often praised by some who are afraid to hurt us.

Help us, like him, to offer those whom you have given to our care the kind of food that endures to eternal life; for this is why you have set your seal on us.

LORD, we often feel deeply hurt when we realise that people are coming to us because we have given them something; they haven't got the message that we need to be loved for our own sake. We thank you that Jesus can understand because he had the same experience.

LORD, we thank you for moments of deep prayer when we know that we have eaten bread from heaven and feel a great calm, as if we will never be hungry or thirsty again.

LORD, great leaders are like Jesus. They don't give in to those who are looking for quick answers to the question, 'What should we do?'
Nor are they intimidated by the challenge, 'What sign will you give to show us that we should believe in you?'
Nor do they try to emulate some Moses of the past who people say gave them bread from heaven to eat; they trust in the truth of their message and the sense that they are doing our work.

Lord, we think of young people today, hungry and thirsty for happiness, deep friendships, meaningful work, prosperity.

If someone promises them these things, they hope for a miracle and cry out excitedly as the people did to Jesus, 'Sir, give us that bread always.'

Help them, Lord, to see that it isn't as easy as that; they must put aside their own desires and give themselves to Jesus, putting all their trust in his values, and then, paradoxically, their hungers and thirsts will be satisfied.

Lord, there are millions of people going hungry today, and we Christians accept this as inevitable; we forget your promise that if we came to Jesus and believed in his teachings the world would never be hungry or thirsty again.

Lord, we long for miraculous bread that will come down from heaven and give life to the world.

You call us back to the reality that bread from heaven is here before our eyes, as truly as Jesus was present to the people.

✳ ✳ ✳ ✳ ✳

John 6:41-51

41Meanwhile the Jews were complaining to each other about him, because he had said, 'I am the bread that has come down from heaven.' 42They were saying, 'Surely this is Jesus son of Joseph, whose father and mother we know. How can he now say, "I have come down from heaven?"' 43Jesus said in reply to them, 'Stop complaining to each other.'

⁴⁴No one can come to me
unless drawn by the Father who sent me,
and I will raise that person up
      on the last day.
⁴⁵It is written in the prophets:
They will all be taught by God;
everyone who has listened to the Father,
and learnt from him,
comes to me.
⁴⁶Not that anybody has seen the Father,
except him who has his being from God:
he has seen the Father.
⁴⁷In all truth I tell you,
everyone who believes has eternal life.
⁴⁸I am the bread of life.
⁴⁹ Your fathers ate manna in the desert
and they are dead;
⁵⁰ but this is the bread
      which comes down from heaven,
so that a person may eat it and not die.
⁵¹I am the living bread
      which has come down from heaven.
Anyone who eats this bread
      will live for ever;
and the bread that I shall give
is my flesh, for the life of the world.'

In this passage, Jesus again draws lessons about life from the feeding of the five thousand.

I remind you that all teaching of Jesus recorded in the gospels is intended to speak to experience and we must therefore appeal to our experience to discover its truth.

As I mentioned earlier, you will find it difficult to do this with passages like these, as I am sure you will discover for yourself. One reason is that the language is not the kind that we use ordinarily, 'eternal life' for example that we met already, or other expressions that we meet for the first time in the chapter, like 'being drawn by the Father, 'living bread' and 'flesh'. You must bring these expressions down to earth for yourself, applying them to what you have lived yourself.

There is, however, a more important reason why you will find the passage difficult to relate to experience and it is simply that it is deep teaching, speaking of a level of experience that we don't reflect on, because we all tend to live at the surface of ourselves.

In meditating on these passages then, you must remember deep experiences. You will naturally think of deep conversion for example, a retreat that changed your life, a life-in-the-Spirit seminar or a prayer moment that you have never forgotten.

But you need not stay with prayer moments; you could think of other deep experiences, a movement for example, or a leader who touched your life. The passage will help you understand these experiences and put them in the context of your growth as a person.

As always with gospel stories, you can focus on the person of Jesus, letting him remind you of someone very important to you and in the process, of the kind of person you yourself would like to be; or then you can focus on the journey the people were called to make, recognising a journey that you or people you love are making or have made.

Remember also that the fruit of your meditation is that you find yourself repeating the actual words of the passage prayerfully and with great gratitude to God for his grace.

It is not possible to meditate deeply on a passage like this all together; you must divide it up and take one section at a time. In fact you will usually find that one section is all you can go into over a week, although you may be able to connect the other sections after a time.

I would suggest the following divisions:

- *Verses 41 to 44* describe a journey that Jesus invites the people to make. In 41 and 42 they are 'complaining': their lives are so ordinary that God could not possibly be with them. All they can see is 'the son of Joseph' whose father and mother 'they knew'.

  In verses 43 and 44 Jesus asks them to look beyond that same ordinary reality and recognise two things: first that their meeting with him is not by chance, but by God's grace, and second that it is a meeting with very great significance, not merely here and now, but for all eternity.

  What encounter in your own experience resulted in your making that kind of journey? What kind of leader is able to challenge people to make one?

- *Verses 45 and 46* speak of a similar journey, this time as one of 'hearing' or 'being taught' or 'learning'. We can know right teaching, but in an abstract way; when we come to Jesus we learn God's lessons personally as if he had taken us aside and given us individual tutoring. Identify a moment when you made that journey and who was the Jesus you 'came to'.

  Verse 46 makes an interesting comment on the process: we don't have to have seen God, only the one who came from God.

- *Verse 47:* Take verse 47 by itself as a reflection on a fact of life. 'Believes' is left vague, and so you are free to take it in as wide a sense as you want of any act of faith. On the other hand, take it to refer to real faith.

  Think of people who have risked their lives, their

careers or friendships for the sake of non-violence or for the liberation of oppressed people or for honesty. Remembering them, you gradually discover the meaning of 'having eternal life' and you will feel a kind of awe as he reflected on the power of that kind of faith, 'I tell you most solemnly'.

Remember world-famous people but don't limit yourself to them; remember members of your own family or your village community.

A negative way of appreciating this powerful verse would be to reflect on the emptiness of a life without faith.

'If a man hasn't discovered something that he will die for, he isn't fit to live' (Martin Luther King).

- In *verses 48 to 50* Jesus speaks of himself as bread. This is a metaphor that is quite frequent in the Bible to describe the teaching of a leader.

  Jesus makes a distinction between two kinds of teacher or leader. There are those who when they find people in a wilderness are content to give them manna after which they die. Jesus is a different kind of teacher: through his teaching people are set free from within themselves so that they live. His teaching gives unlimited depth to a person's life.

- In *verse 51* the teaching is repeated but Jesus makes a new point which he will make clearer in the following passage: the bread he gives is his flesh. Make sure you bring this expression down to experience.

  'Flesh' in Bible language means various things. Here it clearly stresses that Jesus is a source of life by giving himself, not abstract teaching but his own self-sacrificing love. The word goes deeper and says that Jesus did not give himself in power but in weakness and this of course is a tremendous lesson about giving life to others.

Gospel Prayers

LORD, we often complain about
- our bad health, our failures
- the friends who let us down, our parish community
- society today with its materialism, its selfishness, its crimes.

How can anybody say that you are with us?
But Jesus tells us to stop complaining; unless you were drawing us we would not be where we are; the people we live with, the situation we find ourselves in are your gift to us and they can raise us up to your presence. In fact they can raise us up on the last day.

Our prayer has had a beginning because we have had a beginning. But it will have no end. It will accompany us into eternity and will be completed in our contemplation of God.
Carlo Carretto
LORD, we thank you for moments of deep prayer, we can only come to them because you draw us there and we know that they will take us beyond the last day.

LORD, we thank you, those of us who preach the Word, for calling us to be part of this mystery.
People are there, listening to us as they listen to other speakers, but they cannot really come to us unless you draw them. On the other hand, those words of ours, poor though they may be, can raise them up so high that they are beyond the reach of death and all that can harm them.

EUCHARIST AS WORD

LORD, we have known Jesus all our lives, but for a long time he was someone far away, who taught abstract truths. Then, one day, we experienced conversion and it was as if we understood life for the first time. We understood, then, what was written in the prophets, 'They will all be taught by God.'

Teachings that had seemed abstract, we now heard addressed personally to us, and we really learnt from them. That is what it means to come to Jesus. We know that no one has seen you, but we have met the one who came from you and has seen you.

[Gandhi's] impact is not to be measured over two years, or four years or twenty years; the ideas he has given us are imperishable.

A disciple of Gandhi

LORD, how true it is that one who believes has an eternal life. When we put our trust in absolute values – truth, justice, the equality of all men and women, the care of little ones – we are taken out of ourselves, out of our present history and become part of eternity.

LORD, many people take it for granted that their destiny is to be inferior to others
- they will always fail
- they will never overcome their faults
- they will remain forever in bondage.

There are leaders who encourage this attitude, content to give people bread in their wilderness and let them die there. Lord, send us leaders, spiritual guides, like Jesus, who will give us a different kind of teaching, feeding us with another kind of bread, one that comes from you, and helps us to experience that we have it within us to be free and creative, that we are born, not to die in bondage, but to live forever.

LORD, our culture leads us to think that people can only help others from their power, their wealth, or their achievements. We have even come to think that Jesus helped people like that. But the bread that he gave others to eat was his weakness, his flesh
- he made himself vulnerable to children
- he asked the woman at the well for water and Zacchaeus for hospitality
- on the cross he was so human, so much 'flesh' that the good thief could speak words of encouragement to him.

It is by sharing our weakness that we give life to others.
Lord, we thank you for our mothers. They gave us their flesh that we might live.

LORD, our churches are big and beautifully decorated, with imposing statues. But the heart of all is Jesus under the form of simple bread. It is still true that he gives his flesh for the life of the world.

LORD, we pray for our leaders, in Church and state. Teach them that they cannot give life to others by their words but only by giving their flesh.

John 6:51-58

[51]I am the living bread
 which has come down from heaven.
Anyone who eats this bread
 will live for ever;
and the bread that I shall give
is my flesh, for the life of the world.

[52]Then the Jews started arguing among themselves, 'How can this man give us his flesh to eat?' [53]Jesus replied to them:

In all truth I tell you,
if you do not eat
 the flesh of the Son of man
and drink his blood,
you have no life in you.
[54]Anyone who does eat my flesh
 and drink my blood
has eternal life,
and I shall raise that person up
 on the last day.
[55]For my flesh is real food
and my blood is real drink.
[56]Whoever eats my flesh
 and drinks my blood
lives in me
and I live in that person.
[57]As the living Father sent me
and I draw life from the Father,
so whoever eats me
 will also draw life from me.
[58]This is the bread
 which has come down from heaven;
it is not like the bread our ancestors ate:
they are dead,
but anyone who eats this bread
 will live for ever.

This is the fourth extract from John 6 that the Church invites us to meditate on at this time of the year, and the third in which Jesus gives the people a teaching based on their experience of the miraculous feeding.

Some themes are repeated in all the passages and yet each passage has its own dominant theme running through it. In the two previous passages, Jesus presented himself to the people as 'bread come down from heaven'. In this one, he pushes the metaphor further: he gives them his flesh to eat and his blood to drink.

You will find the metaphor strange, but you should try to enter into it, so that it becomes part of your prayer. Remember that in Bible meditation it is not sufficient to get the meaning of a passage; you must get into the words themselves and grow to love them so that you feel moved to repeat them many times.

This metaphor, which – as I have said – you may find difficult at first, has its origins in 'flesh and blood', the biblical expression that means the reality of a human being, with a special stress on his or her weakness or limitations. For example, when in Matthew 16 Peter made his act of faith, it did not come from 'flesh and blood', but as a gift from God. So, too, St Paul warned the Ephesians that their struggle was not merely against 'flesh and blood', but against heavenly forces.

Therefore, when Jesus says that he gives his flesh to eat and his blood to drink, he is saying three things. The first is that he gives himself totally to others; every part of his being is at their service. It is the same as saying, 'This is my body given for you'.

Secondly, he is inviting people to deep union with himself, to 'have his spirit coursing through their souls so that they can know the passion of his love for every one' as we sing in the hymn 'To be the Body of the Lord'.

Thirdly, he wants them to unite their weakness and their sufferings with his so that they can experience his strength and his courage. As he would say to them at the

Last Supper, 'In the world you will have trouble, but be brave, I have conquered the world.' When we eat his flesh and drink his blood, our own flesh and blood are ennobled. St Paul says it in 2 Corinthians: 'We carry with us in our body the death of Jesus so that the life of Jesus too may always be seen in our body.'

The passage is therefore a meditation on Jesus as teacher, leader and guide. In all three roles he does not stand outside of people, he wants to share their lives and to have them share his.

Now this tells us something about God; whereas we tend to imagine God in heaven looking down on us but not getting involved in the movement of our history, Jesus shows God entering into flesh and blood with us. But the passage also tells us about human relationships; in your meditation remember with gratitude people who have been Jesus for you – a parent, a spiritual guide, a friend, a national leader. Naturally you will feel the passage calling you to growth in your own relationships.

Finally a good meditation on this passage will help you to appreciate the Eucharist. It will show you why Jesus chose to be present in the Church under the form of bread and wine.

As I have said before, it is not possible to meditate deeply on a passage like this all together. You must take one section at a time and enter into it, letting it speak to your experience. I suggest the following divisions:

- *Verses 51 and 52:* the people are questioning the very possibility of someone giving himself totally, as Jesus claims to do. Their response is cynical, but is it not typical of the way many would respond today?

- *Verse 53* invites us to think of people who have no life in them, and to go to the root cause: they have never experienced, or perhaps let themselves experience, the kind of selfless love that Jesus gives.

- *Verse 54* introduces the theme we have met several times in the chapter; deep relationship with God in Jesus lifts us up beyond the limitations of time and history.

- In *verse 55* we remember that there is false food and drink and to recognise them we can look at what relationship with Jesus does to us.

- *Verse 56* teaches us the effect of love, the love of Jesus, as well as of all those who love selflessly.

- In *verse 57* we see another effect of selfless love. Here, as frequently in St John's Gospel, Jesus' relationship with his followers is similar to his relationship with his Father – 'As the Father has sent me so I am sending you; as the Father loves me so I have loved you'.

- In *verse 58* we see again the theme of the newness of Jesus' teaching.

Gospel Prayers

LORD, we remember with gratitude the day when we realised for the first time that following Jesus meant eating his flesh and drinking his blood. Up to then, it was a matter of believing abstract truths – that Jesus was truly God and truly man, that there were three persons in

God and seven sacraments. That kind of faith was not a source of life for us.

Then one day we knew that we had to lay down our lives
- caring for a wayward child
- working for reconciliation in the work place so that we were attacked by both workers and employers
- forgiving someone who had hurt us deeply.

At that moment, we knew that Jesus on the cross was present within us, and the strange thing was that we felt an inner strength and freedom, and we were certain that no matter how low we fell he would raise us up.

LORD, self-centredness has become like a first principle of living today. People will argue with one another that it is not even possible for us to give our flesh to be eaten, and yet there can be no life in the world without selfless giving, not in nature, nor in families, nor in any society.

LORD, we pray for those who are mourning for a loved one. Remind them that Jesus gave them his flesh to eat and his blood to drink and he will raise them up on the last day.

I should like to set down here my own belief. In so far as I am willing to be made an instrument of God's peace, in that far have I already entered into eternal life.
Alan Paton

LORD, we thank you for those who eat the flesh and drink the blood of Jesus and therefore already have eternal life.

We need the eyes of deep faith to see Christ in the broken bodies and dirty clothes under which the most beautiful one among the sons of men hides.
Mother Teresa

LORD, help us to receive Jesus when he comes to us in flesh and blood.

LORD, you give us food and drink so that we might live more freely and creatively.
Yet we nourish ourselves with many things that are not life-giving at all, but rather clutter up our lives and keep us in bondage.
We pray that your Christ may be Jesus today, giving the world real food and drink.

LORD, we thank you for the people who have touched our lives; when we read the story of Jesus, we see them living in him, and when we remember their stories, we see Jesus living in them. Truly they have eaten his flesh and drunk his blood.

LORD, we speak too much when we pray. Teach us to remain silent so that we become conscious of Jesus present within us and the life he draws from you may well up in us too.

LORD, we think today of those who see their spouses destroying themselves with bitterness, envy and false pride. With anguish in their hearts, they say to them, as Jesus said to his followers, 'Unless you allow yourself to receive my selfless love, you will not have life within you.'

LORD, we pray for the people of South Africa, Ireland, India, Sri Lanka, the Middle East. For generations, their ancestors have eaten the bread of suspicion, fear and hatred, and they are dead. We thank you that you are raising up new leaders in those countries, and they, like Jesus, are offering their people a different kind of nourishment, based on reconciliation and sharing, bread come down from heaven, so that they can eat it and live.

🝙 🝙 🝙 🝙 🝙

John 6:60-69

60After hearing it, many of his followers said, 'This is intolerable language. How could anyone accept it?' 61Jesus was aware that his followers were complaining about it and said, 'Does this disturb you? 62What if you should see the Son of man ascend to where he was before?

63It is the spirit that gives life,
the flesh has nothing to offer.
The words I have spoken to you are spirit
and they are life.

64But there are some of you who do not believe.' For Jesus knew from the outset who did not believe and who was to betray him. 65He went on, 'This is why I told you that no one could come to me except by the gift of the Father.' 66After this, many of his disciples went away and accompanied him no more. 67Then Jesus said to the Twelve, 'What about you, do you want to go away too?' 68Simon Peter answered, 'Lord, to whom shall we go? You have the message of eternal life, 69and we believe; we have come to know that you are the Holy One of God.'

This is the final extract from John 6 that the Church invites us to meditate on. We have had three rather abstract passages and, no doubt, you will be relieved to find yourself with a story again, just as you had at the opening of the chapter.

The story has different characters. In your meditation, listen carefully to yourself, and you will find that you are reading the passage from the perspective of one of them; stay with that perspective so that you enter the story personally.

There is, first of all, Jesus, and you might like to focus on him as he relates with the other characters. Watch his inner freedom. Already, in the account of the feeding, we saw him sitting on the hillside allowing the people to come to him out of their own freedom.

So too, here, he gives each group their space, those who reject him as well as the twelve – including the betrayer. He also tells us the secret of his inner freedom: he knows he is in his Father's hands and no one can come to him unless the Father allows it.

It is notable, too, that this inner freedom gives him the space to see others clearly, so that he is not deceived by people.

Let your memories of great people who have touched your life confirm the truth of St John's account of Jesus and, of course, let him reveal to you how God wishes to relate with us.

Jesus' words in verse 62 are difficult, but you might want to remain with them. 'The Son of Man ascending to where he was before', probably refers to the painful journey through the passion which would test his followers to the utmost.

Jesus, then, is the great leader who gives his followers a first test and judges whether they will survive the greater ones that lie ahead.

Every word of the great confession of Peter is important; the four statements are various aspects of the one deep commitment. What memories does this stir in you?

Make sure not to be self-righteous as you read of those who rejected Jesus. They symbolise us when we find some demand of God difficult to accept. The use of the word 'language' is significant. When our values go astray we find the language of true believers alien to us.

The mention of the traitor might touch you. Judas is the symbol of the betrayal of Christian values that remains within every community, and within each of us.

Finally, there are the two sayings in verse 63 that are the kind of difficult sayings that occur several times in the chapter.

As I have already urged you to do, be creative in your interpretation, asking yourself when you have experienced the truth of the sayings. 'Flesh', here, is whatever in our lives or in our Church lacks the true spirit of Jesus and therefore is not life-giving in the deepest sense.

The second saying invites us to remember 'words' that gave us life and to see how they could be considered 'spirit'.

Gospel Prayers

LORD, it sometimes happens that when we stand up for our values our companions stop going with us
- because we will not discriminate against people of a different race
- we refuse to give expressions of love that are not appropriate to a relationship
- we criticise those in authority.

Help us, Lord, when this happens, not to become bitter nor to give up our values, but to understand, as Jesus did, that we cannot force people to come to us and that a relationship will only develop if you allow it.

LORD, we thank you for all the times in recent years when your Church has spoken out against injustice in different countries of the world, even when many of its members found this language intolerable and could not accept it.

LORD, we remember the time when we were upset because, for the first time, Jesus asked something hard of us. Now, looking back on it, we smile. What if we had known then how much is entailed in following him on his way to you?

LORD, we live at the surface of ourselves, and so we lack energy and creativity. Give us the grace to withdraw, from time to time, to the depths of ourselves. Only if we go to the level of the spirit can we really live.

LORD, many preachers are content to repeat what they have heard from others. We thank you for those whose words have been life to us because they speak from the depths of their experience.

LORD, forgive us, your Church, that we take pride in our great achievements
• the big numbers that attend our services
• our influence with the rich and the powerful
• our imposing buildings and prestigious institutions,
forgetting that the flesh has nothing to offer.
What will give life to the world is simplicity, truth, compassion, reverence for little people – all that we know to be the spirit of Jesus.

LORD, we thank you for that great moment when we knew we had made a life commitment
- we met the person we should spend the rest of our life with
- we gave our whole selves to a movement
- we read the life of a great person and were never the same afterwards.

We knew then that there was nowhere else for us to go, this was, for us, the way to eternal life. We believed and we knew that this was the Holy One of God. It was like that when people met Jesus.

LORD, to achieve anything worthwhile in life, we have to take risks. We must go ahead and choose twelve, even though one of them eventually betrays us.

LORD, there was a time when we made a deep act of faith and became complacent. We thank you that you sent Jesus to us
- a friend pointed out how self-righteous we had become
- we fell into a sin we thought we had finished with.

This was Jesus reminding us that the capacity to betray him is always part of us too.

LORD, send us leaders like Jesus who will proclaim their message even if many of their followers find the language intolerable and impossible to accept, who will be free enough to turn even to their closest companions and say, 'What about you, do you want to go away too?'

❋ ❋ ❋ ❋ ❋